# How Governme[nt]
## *The Three Bra[nches]*

Lisa A. Klobuchar

## Contents

Rigby
A Harcourt Achieve Imprint

www.Rigby.com
1-800-531-5015

# The Need for Rules and Laws

Think about what it would be like to live in a place where people could do anything they wanted at any time. Everyone might get along for a short while, but sooner or later, there would probably be disagreements. So how do groups of people avoid such trouble? They form governments. The United States government formed in 1787 and is still in place today!

People form governments to work out their problems

## What Is a Government?

A government is a system of rules and laws that tells people how they should and should not behave. A government is made up of the people who make these laws and people who make sure the laws are obeyed.

## Keeping the Peace

The main purpose of a government is to help groups of people to live together peacefully. Governments protect people by making rules and laws.

Police officers make sure laws are followed.

# The United States Government

The government of the United States is made up of three **branches,** or parts. These branches are the legislative branch, the executive branch, and the judicial branch.

## *Separate Jobs*

Each government branch has its own job to do. The legislative branch makes the laws. The executive branch makes sure that people obey the laws. The judicial branch decides whether the laws follow the Constitution of the United States.

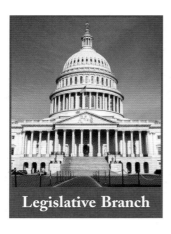

**Legislative Branch**

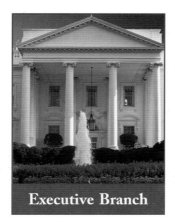

**Executive Branch**

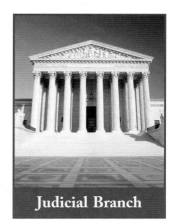

**Judicial Branch**

# *The Constitution of the United States*

The Constitution of the United States is a document, or piece of writing, that describes how the government of the United States works. It sets up the three branches of the U.S. government. It was written in 1787. It states the government's goals and purposes and guides the writing of laws. It describes what powers the government has and does not have. It also lists the people's rights. The government and all Americans must follow the Constitution.

## Goals and Purposes of the U.S Constitution

★ to make sure the country stays together

★ to make sure that rules and laws are applied fairly to all people

★ to allow all people to live together peacefully

★ to protect the country against enemies

★ to protect people's freedoms and happiness

# The Legislative Branch

The legislative branch of the U.S. government is made up of two groups: the House of Representatives and the Senate. Together, these groups are known as Congress.

## Representatives and Senators

The House of Representatives, or House, is the larger group in Congress. Its members are called representatives. The Senate is the smaller group in Congress. Its members are called senators.

### Qualifications for Representatives

* They must be at least 25 years old.
* They must have been a U.S. citizen for the past 7 years.
* They must live in the state they represent.

Representatives are elected for 2-year terms.

### Qualifications for Senators

* They must be at least 30 years old.
* They must be a U.S. citizen for the past 9 years.
* They must live in the state they represent.

Senators are elected for 6-year terms.

# Choosing Members of the Legislative Branch

The people of each state **elect** their representatives and senators. Each state elects a different number of representatives to Congress. States with more people send more representatives than states with fewer people. Each state elects two senators no matter how many people live in the state.

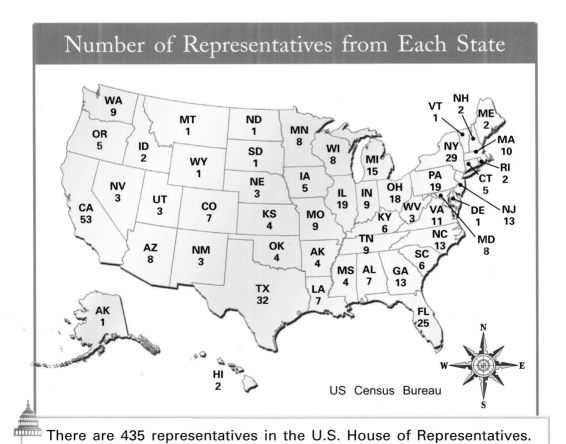

## Number of Representatives from Each State

US Census Bureau

There are 435 representatives in the U.S. House of Representatives.

# The Legislative Branch at Work

The most important work of the legislative branch is making the laws of the United States. These laws deal with every part of life. For example, some laws say how and where highways are built. Other laws tell how schools are run. There are laws to control how mail is delivered and how to give orders to the military.

Laws decide how mail is delivered.

Congress meets every year to discuss new laws.

Representatives and Senators meet separately. Each year they look at more than 10,000 **bills** or proposals for new laws.

Senators and representatives also spend a lot of time working with the **citizens** of their states. They ask them what their needs are and try to help them.

# The Executive Branch

The president of the United States heads the executive branch. The executive branch includes the vice president, and members of the cabinet, too. The cabinet is made up of people who lead the 15 major departments of the government. These people, called secretaries, help the president make rules and run the country's government. Some executive departments include Defense, Education, and Homeland Security.

The cabinet helps the president run the government.

# *Choosing Members of the Executive Branch*

The people of the United States elect the president and the vice president. The president then chooses the secretaries and the heads of the agencies in the executive branch. The Senate must approve these people before they can take office and begin working.

## Qualifications for President and Vice President

★ He or she must be at least 35 years old.

★ He or she must be a natural-born U.S. citizen.

★ He or she must have lived in the U.S. for at least 14 years.

The president and vice president are elected for a 4-year term. The president can only serve two terms. There is no term limit for the vice president.

# The Executive Branch at Work

The president has many jobs and duties. The president makes sure **federal** laws are followed. The president works with Congress to pass bills he or she supports and may also **veto** bills approved by Congress.

The president serves as the leader of the armed forces and also signs treaties with other countries.

The president works with Congress to pass bills.

The president meets with the cabinet and heads of executive departments.

Executive departments and agencies are in charge of carrying out the laws.

Executive departments and agencies have many ways of making sure laws are followed. These might involve carrying out inspections, writing reports, or issuing permits.

# The Judicial Branch

The court system, headed by judges, makes up the judicial branch.

There are two levels of courts in the United States. The Supreme Court, which was created by the Constitution, is the highest court in the country. The federal courts, or lower courts, were created by Congress and are found throughout the country.

The Supreme Court was created by the Constitution.

# *Choosing Members of the Judicial Branch*

The president chooses all federal judges and Supreme Court judges, called justices. The Senate must approve these choices. Federal and Supreme Court justices remain in office for life unless they are found guilty of a crime.

## Qualifications for Federal Judges and Supreme Court Justices

★ There are no official qualifications for judges.

★ Most judges have been trained in the law.

★ Judges and justices are appointed for life.

Currently, there are nine justices on the Supreme Court.

# The Judicial Branch at Work

The judicial branch of the government decides what the laws mean, how the laws should be carried out, and whether the laws follow the rules of the Constitution. Judges settle disagreements between people or between people and the government. Judges make sure that the laws are followed by all people.

# Federal Courts

The two main types of federal courts are **trial** courts and courts of **appeal**. Trial courts hear cases, or problems that are brought to court, for the first time. The side that loses a case in a trial court can take the case to a court of appeal. The court of appeal then decides whether the trial court's decision was correct or not.

Cases first go to trial court.

## The Supreme Court

The most important job of the Supreme Court is to decide if a law or government action is unconstitutional. The Constitution describes the kinds of laws that the government can and cannot make. A law is unconstitutional if it does something that the Constitution says it cannot do. The Supreme Court's rulings can overturn the rulings of any lower court. The Supreme Court has the final say on all laws.

The Supreme Court can change laws.

# Checks and Balances

Each branch of the federal government has different powers and jobs. This helps the government run smoothly. More importantly, these separate powers keep one branch of the government from becoming more powerful than the other branches. This system of separate powers is called checks and balances. Checks and balances means that each branch of the government has the power to stop another branch from doing something it does not agree with.

Checks and balances help to make sure that all branches of government have equal power. The scale represents the idea of checks and balances.

## Examples of Checks and Balances

| Job | Legislative Check | Executive Check | Judicial Check |
|---|---|---|---|
| **Congress passes a bill.** | Both the Senate and House of Representatives must agree to the same bill. | President can sign or veto the bill. | The Supreme Count can rule a law to be unconstitutional. |
| **President vetoes a bill.** | Congress can vote to stop the veto. | | |
| **The Supreme Court rules a law is unconstitutional.** | Congress, along with the states, can amend, or change the Constitution. | | |
| **The Supreme Court finds a person guilty of a crime.** | | President can let the person go free. | |

# How a Bill Becomes a Law

## Introducing a Bill

An idea for a law can begin with anyone. Then a member of Congress presents it to the House or Senate for review. Then the bill goes to a House or Senate committee, or group where certain members take a closer look at the idea. In the following example, the bill starts in the Senate.

## Writing a Bill

Members of the committee work on writing the bill. The committee then presents the bill to the full Senate for a vote.

A Senator introduces the bill in the Senate.

Committee members look at the bill.

All of the senators vote.

## Passing a Bill

If more than half of the senators vote for the bill, it goes to the House. The bill goes through the same process it did in the Senate. If the House votes to pass the bill, it then goes to a special committee that makes sure that the forms of the bill passed in both the Senate and House are exactly the same.

## On to the President

The bill is then sent to the president. If the president agrees with the bill it becomes a law. If the president disagrees with the bill, he or she may veto it. However, Congress can stop the president's veto if two-thirds of both houses vote to make the bill become a law anyway.

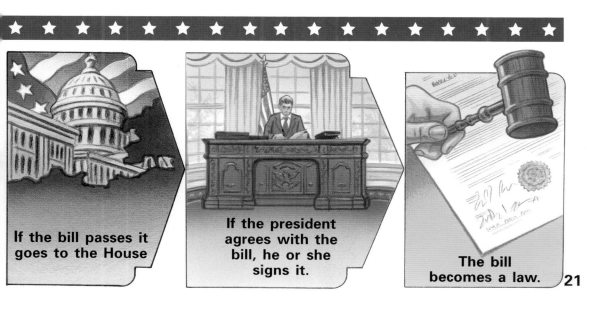

If the bill passes it goes to the House

If the president agrees with the bill, he or she signs it.

The bill becomes a law.

21

## Testing the Law

People who do not like the law may question it by taking it to court. The courts decide whether the law is constitutional. The Supreme Court has the final say on all laws. If a law is found to be unconstitutional, it will not be a law anymore. However, Congress can start the process over again by introducing a new, similar bill.

Every American has the right to question laws.

## Government and You

Now you've seen how the government works! There are many different parts, but they all work together to make sure everything runs smoothly.

Do you think you might want to work for the government some day? What branch would you most like to work in? Maybe one day you will work in the judicial branch as a Supreme Court justice who decides important cases. Maybe you would rather be in the legislative branch as a senator who helps the people who live in your state. Or, if you choose the executive branch, maybe you will become the President of the United States!

Maybe one day there will be a statue of you!

# Glossary

**appeal** to ask a court to change a decision that a lower court has made

**bill** a suggested idea for a law

**branches** the parts of a government

**citizens** people who live in a certain place

**elect** to choose someone for a job by voting for him or her

**federal** having to do with the national government

**trial** the legal process in which a judge and jury listen to arguments and decide if a person is guilty of a crime

**unconstitutional** going against the United States Constitution

**veto** to say no

# Index